the

unexpected

joy of

being

sober

journal

the
unexpected
joy of
being
sober
journal

· · · ● ● ● ●   ● ● ● · · ·

your intentions ● your journey ● your joy

catherine gray

aster

DEDICATION

For all the hedonists, party animals, ragers, boozehounds, caners and barflies out there.

You are My People.

I get you. I feel you. I understand why. I still am you.

I'm just powered by herbal tea and yoga these days, rather than booze and contraband third-glass-of-wine fags.

Come see what sober really feels like. Then you can decide which life you prefer.

An Hachette UK Company
www.hachette.co.uk

First published in Great Britain in 2018 by Aster, an imprint of Octopus Publishing Group Ltd
Carmelite House,
50 Victoria Embankment
London EC4Y 0DZ
www.octopusbooks.co.uk

ISBN 978-1-78325-308-1

A CIP catalogue record for this book is available from the British Library.

Printed and bound in Italy

10 9 8 7 6 5 4 3 2 1

Publishing director
   Stephanie Jackson
Senior editor Pauline Bache
Art director Yasia Williams-Leedham
Designer Sally Bond
Picture library manager
   Jennifer Veall
Picture research manager
   Giulia Hetherington
Production manager
   Caroline Alberti

CONTENTS

Dogs don't drink
and they love life.

@ @unexpectedjoyof

FEEL FREE TO SNAP AND SHARE ON INSTAGRAM/TWITTER/FACEBOOK.
IF YOU'RE NOT ON THE SOCIALS (RESPECT!), CUT IT OUT, PUT IT IN YOUR WALLET, WHATEVER WORKS.

PREFACE:
NOT DRINKING IN A MOSTLY DRINKING WORLD

If you're reading this, you're likely embarking upon, or have already commenced, an alcohol-free mission, whether for four weeks or forevermore. And for that, I applaud you. Mentally, I'm giving you a high five right now. Because it takes serious courage to peel away from the pack, stop conforming, and say 'no ta' in a mostly drinking world.

It's much easier to just continue drinking, despite the irony that drinking often makes life *harder*.

It's easier to say 'yes' than 'no'.

It's easier not to scrutinize your drinking too closely, to just carry on regardless, to snuggle deeper into denial.

By quitting, for however long, you are doing a commendable, hard and nerve-wracking thing.

Five years ago I realized I was hopelessly addicted to alcohol, and that if I wanted to keep my friends, family, health, sanity and income, it was definitely the most sensible decision for me to quit. Medically speaking, I was apparently fine, but I felt like I was slowly dying.

Despite only having been awarded one body, I was trashing it like a rock star trashes a hotel room, with lashings of booze, fags, fried chicken and late nights. My alcohol intake had ticked up slowly, slowly, until I was drinking around seven or eight bottles of wine a week, and only taking one or two nights off.

I felt like I was at an impossible crossroads; like I couldn't continue to live with, and yet couldn't live *without* drinking. Exactly like that U2 song. After many months of soul-searching and false starts, of ever-more-scary spells of drinking and peaceful sober stints, I finally realized that I preferred life sober.

Choosing sober would turn out to be the best decision I'd ever made, and yet I embarked upon it feeling like I was committing social suicide. Just as George Michael mournfully sings in *Careless Whisper*, I honestly thought I was never gonna dance again. I felt like I was pawning a bejewelled party dress to get money for my pension. Like I was hawking a vintage record player to pay the electricity bill. *Great*.

And so, when I discovered how much happier, healthier and wealthier I became, I felt like I'd stumbled upon the world's best-kept secret. Sobriety was only one part angst to nine parts wonder. Why did nobody tell me? So, I've been banging on about it ever since. I think people ought to know.

Thousands of my readers have quit drinking too, whether totally or mostly, and have since contacted me to say that they too are much, much happier. That they wish they'd done it years ago. That the rewards far outweigh the 'Aggg, this is so hard' beginning.

The last five sober years have been the best of my life. And I'm not just comparing them to the dark years when I was drinking dependently. No. I'm also comparing them to the brighter years when I was drinking somewhat moderately. And yet sobriety still wins, hands down; it has a royal flush to moderate drinking's pair of jacks.

We live in a mad world when it comes to booze. And it's only once you actually step outside of the drinking world, into the non-drinking one, that you begin to see how bonkers it truly is.

We used to live in a mad world when it came to cigarettes too, and it took a long while for society to achieve sanity – for smoking to no longer be seen as 'cool' or 'relaxing', and for Big Tobacco to be stripped of their sway over our minds and wallets.

I remember chomping on candy cigarettes in the late 1980s; white sugary sticks that were purposely styled to look like real fags. One American manufacturer featured the strapline 'Just like Dad!' with a kid saying 'Hey Dad, can I bum a smoke?'.

That seems horrifying today, that kids were encouraged to aspire to be smokers. But we are living in that *exact place* right now with alcohol. Even from the cradle, drinking is expected, with babygros featuring slogans like 'Daddy's drinking buddy' or 'I drink until I pass out'. I picked up a card in a shop recently that featured a little girl with a pint and the slogan, 'When I grow up, I want to be a binge drinker!' (My niece can now read – and comprehend – these messages aged five years old.)

Meanwhile, liver disease is officially set to overtake heart disease in the UK as the biggest cause of death by 2020. Deaths by liver disease have increased fivefold since the 1970s. Do we really want our kids to think binge drinking is funny? Binge drinking is lethal, not jolly.

We live in a world that pushes us toward drinking (those trying to sell us stuff + each other), and simultaneously pulls us away from drinking (health news + the medical industry). It's no bloody wonder we're confused.

We live in a world where 35 Brits *a day* are expected to die from drinking over the next few years, and yet the alcohol industry is not obliged to put ANY health warnings on booze, aside from the lame, blame-dodging 'drink responsibly'.

You've got to be GIN IT to win it

I walked into a supermarket recently and saw candles saying 'Wine not', greetings cards with 'On your marks, get set, prosecco!' and T-shirts emblazoned with 'You've got to be gin it to win it'. When I reached the pharmacy I saw a sign saying that alcohol is the leading cause of ill health, disability and death among 15–49 year olds in Britain. Stark contrast, no? Disturbing, even.

The reason profit-centred companies slap these messages on candles, cards and T-shirts is because they sell; because so many of us binge drink. Enabling, condoning and endorsing this national pastime makes them pots of money.

Due to booze being a national treasure, one of the hardest things about not drinking is *other people*. We say things to each other like 'You're doing Dry Jan?! Oh, see you in Feb then mate', or 'You don't drink? Awww, you're no fun' (the last thing somebody wants to be called at a party is 'no fun').

We say things like 'I can't be friends with someone who doesn't drink' at parties, and get laughs as a reward (I used to say this kind of twaddle, back when I was a dedicated drinker). When you drink, you don't have to justify why, but when you don't, you often have to give an explanation. 'Why aren't you drinking?!' It's topsy-turvy.

The social pressure to drink is baffling, intense and unfair. When you add this pressure to the surreptitious messages on TV, in advertising, even in gyms (post-class proseccos to 'retox' are often mentioned in my spinning class) and on coasters ('Alcohol! It's cheaper than a psychiatrist!'), it's no surprise that it can be tough to stay off the sauce. We're constantly told, in every imaginable way, that alcohol is relief, fun and relaxation.

This is why oak-strong resolve to *not drink* becomes weakened over time. Personally, we want to *not drink*, but the atmosphere we live in slowly and surely chips away at that resolve.

We need tools to deal with the social pressure. We need to constantly debate the messages we're receiving, rather than passively accepting them. We need to consciously reverse-condition ourselves. Hang onto the reasons we started this sobriety thing in the first place. Wait for the returns on our investment, which, I promise you, will be a hundredfold the initial outlay.

I hope that this journal will help you to do all of these things, whether your alcohol-free mission is for three months or a lifetime.

So, let's get cracking, shall we?

'Stone-cold sober'?
Nah. It should be called
'sunshine-warm sober'.
Because that's what it
actually feels like.

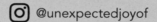 @unexpectedjoyof

get the
teetotal
ball
rolling

TALK TO ME

I've told you a bit about my drinking story; now I want to hear yours.
Come in, sit down, put your feet up, and I'll get us some tea.

So tell me, what does your drinking look like?
Has it started to look different in recent years?

_____

_____

_____

_____

_____

_____

Why do you want to have a booze sabbatical /
quit for good?

_____

_____

_____

_____

_____

_____

_____

Most people bounce into a booze-free period as a result of a scary night, or a soul-crushingly hungover day, or a series of these. If this applies to you, tell me about these nights/days.

What are your worst fears about sobriety?

_____

_____

_____

_____

_____

_____

_____

What are your brightest hopes?

_____

_____

_____

_____

_____

_____

_____

_____

Sober-curious?
You won't know what
it's like until you
actually go there.

@unexpectedjoyof

THERE IS NO SUCH THING AS THE PERFECT TIME

If you're waiting for the 'perfect time' to quit drinking, you will be waiting for-ev-er.

There will always be birthday drinks, a wedding, a wine-tasting, a whatever that rotates around booze, because society *rotates around booze*.

So bite the bullet, my friend. Now's the best time. It will be challenging, but it will also be totally worth it.

Here's what we're going to do. We're going to look at the next thirty days and flag up the events you're worried about. Then you're going to make a plan for how to make this event *as easy for yourself as possible*.

Some ideas from me, but do come up with your own too:

 Exercise beforehand. You'll be much more zen.

 Tell your hosts and all of your friends in attendance, that you won't be drinking, in advance. See page 30 for a ready-made sober announcement.

 Go early and make noises that you'll need to leave early.

 Bring someone to the party who you know will support your non-drinking. Ideally, source a plus one who's also teetotal. I have picked up all my best sober friends from Facebook and Instagram. All you need to do is type in 'Sober' and you'll be deluged by people, hashtags and groups.

 If you want your non-drinking to stay under the radar, rather than have *all the questions*, always have a glass in your hand, filled with something that looks like it could be alcoholic. Elderflower pressé in a wine glass is an excellent diversion. Or alcohol-free beer (check the label, not all are 0% alcohol). Take it with you to the shindig.

 Have a code word or sound for 'Get me the twatting hell out of here before I pounce upon that bottle of wine'. A soft bird call (which nobody will think is strange, for sure). 'Pomegranate' maybe. Or a text saying 'SOS'.

 Do an 'Irish trapdoor' if you've really had enough and can't be arsed with the rigmarole of saying goodbye to everyone and being strong-armed into staying. In other words, just *bounce*.

EVENT ONE

How to make my non-drinking as easy as possible:

_____

_____

_____

_____

EVENT TWO

How to make my non-drinking as easy as possible:

_____

_____

_____

_____

EVENT THREE

How to make my non-drinking as easy as possible:

_____

_____

_____

_____

Once you settle into sobriety, you'll be confident enough to be brazen about your booze-free existence, stay late and even go to parties alone, but for now, do everything you can to support yourself.

Locate your teetotal tribe.
There's joy in numbers.

@unexpectedjoyof

Make a list of ways you could find sober friends, from in-real-life recovery groups to Facebook networking. Then research these options for your area/country, and write a list of friend-finding goldmines to dig around in.

GETTING YOUR HOUSE IN ORDER

You will be infinitely more likely to succeed if you try the following:

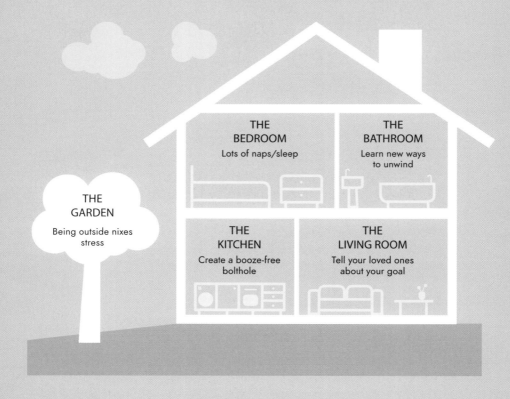

THE GARDEN
Being outside nixes stress

THE BEDROOM
Lots of naps/sleep

THE BATHROOM
Learn new ways to unwind

THE KITCHEN
Create a booze-free bolthole

THE LIVING ROOM
Tell your loved ones about your goal

I don't live in a house like this either, nor do I have a garden, but let's just pretend. This is just your *metaphorical* residence.

There's a recovery acronym called HALT, which has saved my sober skin countless times. It stands for Hungry, Angry, Lonely, Tired. If you're HALT (or even just half of it – HA or AL), then you're much more likely to want to drink/actually drink. This is why self-care is so damn important. Eat, meditate, ask for a hug and nap like your life depends on it.

If you previously used drinking as a segue from clenched to chilled in the evening, you'll need to replace this with new ways of de-stressing. I love to mark the 7pm end of the working day with a bath (followed by PJs and a face mask), a yoga class (or 'noga' as I like to call my yoga), a boxset treat or a takeaway. These ideas are forehead-slappingly obvious, but my point is, if you don't replace this wine/beer/cider segue with something, there will be a gaping hole where a 'treat' should be.

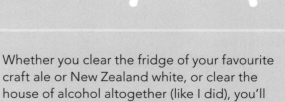

Whether you clear the fridge of your favourite craft ale or New Zealand white, or clear the house of alcohol altogether (like I did), you'll be so much more likely to succeed if you create a temptation-free space.

Keeping people in the dark about your alcohol-free month/three months/lifetime mission starves you of support and accountability. You don't have to tell them *everything*, but do tell them *something*. Ask for help in not drinking. (If they won't help, avoid them, frankly.) On page 30, there's a checklist to help you tell people en masse.

Dozens upon dozens of studies have shown that being around (or even just looking at pictures of) nature can lower stress, reduce blood pressure, soothe trauma, stroke anger – all that magical stuff. So get moving and get outside. Scientists have found that a fierce alcohol craving can be jettisoned by just ten minutes of exercise.

It's 100 times easier to get sober in a dry house.

@unexpectedjoyof

What ideas do you have for de-stressing without alcohol?
Write a big list of tactics you could use, here.

_____

_____

_____

_____

_____

_____

_____

_____

_____

_____

_____

_____

_____

_____

_____

_____

_____

We're meant to dive into lakes to de-stress, not dive into wine.

@unexpectedjoyof

Drinking sucks. Choose cats.

 @unexpectedjoyof

YOUR SOBER SOCIAL ANNOUNCEMENT

Oh hi, friends/family/other animals. I am fed up of the following side effects of drinking:

[TICK AS APPROPRIATE. If your side effects aren't shown, jot them in at the bottom.]

☐ Seventh-circle-of-hell hangovers

☐ Morning-after anxiety (otherwise known as 'beer fear')

☐ Doing shite I can't remember

☐ Lining the pockets of pub landlords across town

☐ Smoking/eating unidentifiable fried items/shopping online while drunk

☐ Feeling like I'm not firing on all cylinders at work

☐ Lack of sleep due to 'just one more drink/bar'

☐ Swerving exercise the day of/after a session

☐ _____

☐ _____

So, I am going totally sober for:

☐ One month

☐ Three months

☐ Six months

☐ A year

☐ Forevermore

☐ None of the above
Insert time-frame _____
(or simply 'as long as I blinking well
feel like it')

Please be a legend and help me achieve my goal by:

☐ Congratulating me rather than saying *hilarious* things like 'you're now dead to me'.

☐ Offering me an alcohol-free drink when you go to the bar (you'll be amazed how often teetotallers get forgotten in rounds).

☐ Telling me if you notice nice physical/ character changes in me. I'm trying hard, so please tell me of any positives.

☐ Still seeing me just as often. Inviting me to nights out. I am not now socially irrelevant.

☐ Not giving me a speech about how easy you find it to moderate (if you do). Good for you, but please, button it for now.

☐ If we are going to meet in the pub, picking a pub where there's great food/board games/a lush garden/pool tables/something other than booze.

☐ Remembering that, given lemonade does not make you want to stay up until 2am, I may want to head home earlier than you.

☐ Knowing that this is zero to do with you, or what's in your glass. Crack on. Drink your fill. I won't judge you. So let's go have some fun.

Trees lower anxiety.
Trees don't give you hangovers.

 @unexpectedjoyof

What else, other than lashings of booze, lowers your anxiety?

_____

_____

_____

_____

_____

There's infinite pleasure to be had without getting smashed.

What gives you
pleasure, with no
alcohol required?
Write a list:

_____

_____

_____

_____

_____

_____

_____

_____

_____

learning the
superpower
of sober
socializing

THE CHEAT CODE
OF ALCOHOL

I'm not going to lie to you. Sober socializing is pretty savage, to begin with.

Here's why. When we're kids, we are generally excited, rather than nervous, about parties. The only real fears we have are sensible adversaries like spiders, thunder, the bogeyman and bananas with 'bits' on.

Then, as adolescents, we grow inhibitions, shyness and a desire to attract people we find sexy. Instead of naturally learning how to deal with these newfound social anxieties, we pick up the alcohol that society thrusts into our hands. Here's the solution! Party – officially started.

Instead of genuinely learning how to go to a party and talk to strangers, do the conga at a wedding or go on a first date and not die of fright, we are given a fast lane, a quick fix.

The alcohol is like a cheat code we enter into a computer game, allowing us to whizz up from level two (socially awkward) to level six (rakish raconteur, who performs running-man dance move for entire kitchenful*). The problem is, we then don't learn how to move through levels three, four and five for real. We're reliant on the cheat code.

*Actual thing I once did, badly.

When the crutch of alcohol is taken away, we have to learn how to do all of our socializing without it. Which isn't easy. It feels clunky to begin with.

Whenever you walk into a party or sit down for a meal, your brain is accustomed to this being the time when you drink alcohol. 'Gimme booze!' it will yell. It will release a cascade of dopamine (the 'wanting' neurotransmitter) in response to the boozy cues around you.

You need to learn how to sit through this discomfort, remember to breathe and trust that it will pass. Which it will do, surprisingly quickly. You'll be amazed how quickly.

Learning how to socialize sober is like learning how to do anything. Speaking a new language, rollerblading, giving a presentation. It takes repetition and time for it to feel comfortable. For a new neural pathway to bed down in your brain. It's been shown that 66 days of repetition is required before a new activity becomes a reflexive habit.

But once you have nailed the art of sober socializing, you've learnt a superpower that you will never un-learn. You're doing what you would have done naturally, as a teen, had drinking not been placed under your nose as a solution. And it feels immensely satisfying, once you get the hang of it.

You'll even feel a little invincible. 'If I can do *that*, what else can I do?'

Tell me, what age were you when you first started drinking? _____

What social purpose did the drinking serve?

_____
_____
_____
_____
_____

Do you think you came to rely on the alcohol for this?

_____
_____
_____
_____
_____
_____
_____

PARTY RELAXATION HACK

Find someone else at the party who is visibly nervous and channel all your energy into putting them at ease. It's social sorcery that works.

SNAP & SHARE

Kids have a blast without booze.

You can too.

@unexpectedjoyof

being able to
SOCIALIZE
WITHOUT
DRINKING
IS LIKE A
superpower

@unexpectedjoyof

Shy is lovely. Shy is perfect.

Don't feel you need to drink your
way out of being shy.

@unexpectedjoyof

THE TEETH-GRITTING COUNTERS

I still have butt-clenchingly bad moments at parties, even at five years sober. It's generally when I feel left out, as a teetotaller.

Champagne flutes being passed around for a toast; a game of beer pong/flip-cup commencing; or the braying and chest-pounding that comes with the social ritual of a round of shots.

But when I count up how long these howlers actually last and look at it in the big picture of the entire night, it gives me perspective.

(The counting also turns it into a game. Love a game.)

During your next four nights out, count the seconds where you feel horribly awkward, due to your non-drinking, and insert the figures inside these clocks.

NIGHT OUT 1

NIGHT OUT 2

NIGHT OUT 3

NIGHT OUT 4

'WELL, THIS IS AWKWARD' STRATEGIES

1 Literally clench your buttocks. I find this extremely, weirdly satisfying. (They'll have a hangover, I'll have a better bum. Firm bum > Ferocious hangover.)

2 Box breathe. Breathe in for seven, hold for seven, out for seven, hold for seven.

3 Go to the loo and rejoice in the porcelain throne of peace.

4 Text somebody about what just happened, turning it into a funny tale.

5 Play flip-cup with sparkling water and slay at it. (I've done this. Who says you can't play flip-cup sober?)

What strategies help you to ride out the awkward moments? Write them down, here.

_____
_____
_____
_____
_____
_____
_____
_____
_____
_____
_____
_____

Wobbling is merely a sign you're doing
a hard thing and getting stronger.

DRINK-PUSHING BINGO

The struggle is real! Many people love to try to capsize sober voyages or sabotage teetotal missions by trying to strong-arm and press-gang you back into drinking. Or they subtly undermine you by blathering on about their apparent ability to moderate (normally while visibly drunk, ironically).

Let's stay sane by turning it into a game. First one to get a full house wins... ummm... a magical sober guardian that is so small you won't be able to see it. But it's there. I'll courier it to your house... via owl post.

BINGO

When is this 'no drinking' nonsense gonna be over?	Can't you just have one? For me? Please?	BOR-INGGGG.
It'd be rude not to.	Everything in moderation, including moderation*.	Me, I just drink because I love the taste (says person on fourth/fifth drink).
But it's Friday!/ my birthday!/ my engagement party!	Frank Sinatra once said 'I feel sorry for people that don't drink, because when they wake up in the morning, that is the best they are going to feel ALL DAY.'	Hitler was teetotal, y'know/ Trump is teetotal, y'know.
But you are still drinking the champagne toast, right?	I could easily stop if I wanted to, but I just don't want to. You only live once, am I right?!	I don't trust people who don't drink!

*Always delivered as if they have thought of something *very* original.

DRINK-PUSHING COMEBACKS

Deliver these with a tip of your alcohol-free glass, a wink and a generous smile.

INSTANT LAUGHS:
'If I drink, I'll be dancing topless on *that* table by midnight. This is safest for everyone, believe me buddy.'

MADE-UP STATS:
'I find that alcohol increases the chances of my doing something regrettable by the power of 1000.'

FAUX HORROR:
'If you think I'm boring sober, I fear our friendship may be in serious peril!'

THOUGHT-PROVOKER:
'I'm craving a happy day, rather than just a happy hour.'

HITLER NONSENSE:
'Hitler was also a despot and a raging cocaine user. Which, happily, I'm not.'

RUDENESS SLINGBACK: 'It'd be rude not to? When I'm smashed I try to smoke inside/chat up inappropriate people/leave half-eaten pizzas around the house/start political debates/break glasses. I'm actually much less rude sober.'

TRUMP CARD:
'I'm nothing like Trump, because I can totally say "anonymous". Anonymous, anonymous, anonymous. See?'
Does a twirl/takes a bow

FAST FUN: 'When Wetherspoon's offered me a loyalty card, I knew it was time for a change.'

ONE-LINER: 'Spies aren't allowed to drink while they're on a mission.'
Dead serious poker face

DIGNITY-REMOVER: 'I find alcohol to be an excellent dignity-remover/ inhibition-remover/energy-remover [delete as appropriate], it's true, but I want to hang onto my dignity/inhibitions/ energy, thanksverymuch.'

YOLO: 'You only live once? I know, right?! So, personally, I don't want to waste another second blackout drunk in a sticky-carpeted nightclub, or lying in bed groaning on a beautifully sunny Saturday morning.'

YOUR OWN IDEAS FOR COMEBACKS:

1 _____
_____

2 _____
_____

3 _____
_____

YOUR MISSION SHOULD YOU CHOOSE TO ACCEPT IT

Sod it, let's pretend you are actually a spy, gathering intelligence at each party.

YOUR TASK is to observe when people are the most interesting/funny/articulate/kind/magnetic. You have a unique perspective now, as a sober onlooker. The veil has been removed and you can see things as they really are.

Personally, I find it's in the first couple of hours of the party, or maybe hours two and three, if it's a disparate group of people who need to bond.

This is in stark contrast to when partygoers *feel like* they're social dynamite or *feel like* they're Beyoncé/ Ryan Gosling, which is after a few jars. The most charming and glowy people are usually the most sober.

This was an eye-opener for me in early sobriety; a realization that powered me into longer-term sobriety.

Go forth and investigate, agent OO-NO-TA. Make notes on your findings, overleaf.

Some questions to have in your back pocket include:

- Observe those who are slightly socially awkward before they've had an alcoholic drink. How do you feel about their initial shyness? (In ourselves, we often denounce shyness as a social failing, but in others, this is often endearing. Usually it makes them even more likeable than somebody who bounces into a party brimming with confidence.)

- What happens to people once they've tipped over the two-drink mark, into the third drink and beyond?

- What negative consequences of alcohol do you observe, over the course of the night? (This could be anything physical or emotional – from a smashed ornament to a couple bickering over 'I want to leave/I want to stay'.)

- Do people talk about boozing/the effects of boozing a lot? (I was amazed when I quit, to observe how much people actually talk about getting smashed/alcohol/being hungover.)

- Do you notice any gaps between how people believe they are being (flirtatious, amusing, clever) and how they are actually being?

- What do you think the alcohol was used for, at the party, by most of the people there? What was the purpose of it?

- Is [insert purpose] achievable naturally?

- Has this recce changed your perceptions of how people *really are* when drunk, vs. how they *feel they are* when drunk?

YOUR SOBER SOCIAL STAKE-OUTS

SOCIAL STAKE-OUT ONE NOTES:

_____

_____

_____

_____

_____

_____

_____

SOCIAL STAKE-OUT TWO NOTES:

_____

_____

_____

_____

_____

_____

_____

SOCIAL STAKE-OUT THREE NOTES:

_____

_____

_____

_____

_____

_____

_____

_____

SOCIAL STAKE-OUT FOUR NOTES:

_____

_____

_____

_____

_____

_____

_____

_____

_____

seeking the
El Dorado of
moderation

THE CYCLICAL MODERATION TRAP

The standard, most common reaction you will get when you tell people you're drinking zero, is 'Why don't you just have one? I can easily just have one!' (This person will then go on to have three drinks, minimum.)

Why? Because moderation is about as easy as herding cats. The very nature of alcohol makes it fiendishly difficult to control, contain and tame.

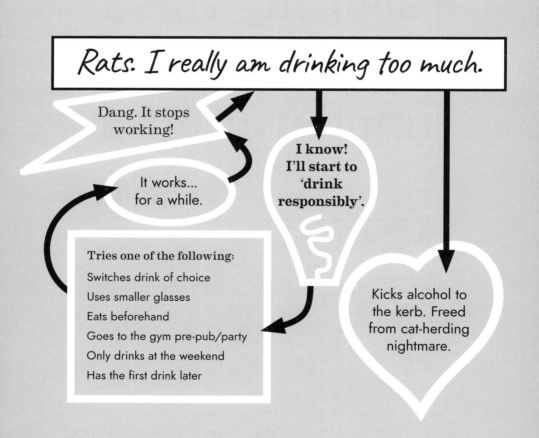

Rats. I really am drinking too much.

Dang. It stops working!

It works... for a while.

I know! I'll start to 'drink responsibly'.

Tries one of the following:

Switches drink of choice

Uses smaller glasses

Eats beforehand

Goes to the gym pre-pub/party

Only drinks at the weekend

Has the first drink later

Kicks alcohol to the kerb. Freed from cat-herding nightmare.

Write here about what tactics you have used in your quest to 'drink responsibly'.

In my opinion (and in the opinion of many experts) it's practically impossible to 'drink responsibly'.

Alcohol is a dis-inhibitor, which means it erases your inhibitions, encouraging impulsive, irrational decisions.

For the lion's share of people, our first one or two drinks literally erase our ability to say 'nah' to the third and fourth.

This is why no drinks are easier than the forever elusive 'one drink'.

NON-MODERATION IS THE NORM

Think you're 'broken' because you can't stop at one or two? On the contrary, friend, you are merely the norm. An average kinda bear. Really.

Traditionally, people just haven't talked about their fears and angst around non-moderation, but that is thankfully beginning to change as the stigma of 'failing' at moderation recedes and people begin to realize that it's actually incredibly difficult to use a highly addictive substance in a non-addictive way.

The biggest study into drinking habits ever undertaken, and published in 2018, found that British men and women are, on average, drinking 26 units a week* (12 units above the NHS recommended cut-off of 14 units).

This finding shows us that we are collectively botching moderation. We're led to believe that non-moderators are the exception, a small minority who just can't do this thing; but we're actually the rule.

*To me that sounds like child's play, mere beginners' drinking, given I was putting away 70–80 units a week at my worst.

How often do/did you successfully moderate (by having one or maximum two drinks), and how often do/did you drink more than that?

_____

_____

_____

Think about your ten closest friends. Do you know anyone who always sticks to one or two drinks per night out? Who never drinks more than they initially intended to?

_____

_____

_____

If you do know someone like that, a lesser-spotted 'responsible drinker', how many people do you know who don't do that?

_____

_____

That gives you a rough ratio of the people you know who can/can't moderate. Insert it below.

_____ **/ 10**

My ratio is that 8/10 of my close friends don't/can't actually moderate.

Once you start drinking, it's difficult to stop. It's like a car that's been released from its handbrake and has started determinedly rolling downhill.

THE REALITY
OF OUR DRINKING

The average British man drinks three drinks a day.

British women clock up, on average, three drinks a day.

65%

GPs guestimate that 65 per cent of us are alcohol dependent.

twice
as much alcohol

Double the amount of alcohol is sold, compared to what people admit they're drinking.

Where is all of this extra purchased alcohol going? Probably mostly down people's necks, without them realizing how much they're putting away.

I don't know anyone with an actual wine cellar, do you? I also don't know anyone with an emergency bunker stuffed to the ceiling with hipster ale, in case the zombie apocalypse hits and craft ale production ceases. And I doubt that those bottles of dodgy green spirits, that sit at the back of spirits cupboards gathering dust, amount to that enormous discrepancy.

Therefore, people are probably hugely underestimating what they're knocking back.

2 years

The average life lost if you drink 21, rather than 14 units a week, is two years. And yes, those might be miserable years spent in 'Sunset Village' retirement home wearing 'adult protection' pads and drooling in front of daytime TV, but you can't know that for sure. They could also be badass twilight years going on cruises to see the northern lights, or tending to the best allotment in all of Yorkshire, or watching your grandkid graduate, or somesuch other elderly person loveliness.

We only get one go on this gorgeous planet, and I want the longest go possible. If you die earlier due to drinking, you won't die abruptly, as if a musical statue, at a party while busting out some moves. 'Live fast, die young' means your body will probably start breaking earlier in life, rather than your merry existence scratching to a sudden stop like a record whipped off a turntable. I don't want *less* life. I want as much as possible.

How about you?

_____

_____

_____

_____

_____

4 in 10 of us

40 per cent of us exceed our weekly 14 units in just one night, on (at least) a monthly basis, said one survey. In my drinking days, I could easily sink a bottle-and-a-half of wine in one night, so yep, I relate to that, hard.

HOW MANY UNITS WERE YOU REALLY PUTTING AWAY?

It's really easy to live in the duvet of drinking denial, forever. It takes bravery and great strength of character to start to contemplate life outside of this duvet. (Yes, I'm talking to you, you little beauty.)

Rather than having someone rip this duvet from us, it's better to inch our way out of it ourselves, which is why interventions are generally a big fat bust.

Start doing so, slowly, by being unflinchingly truthful with yourself about how much you were drinking per week.

Take a recent drinking week, probably a large one, and ruthlessly add up the drinks.

Find out what a unit of alcohol is (you can Google this for more detail, but roughly, a 250ml glass of wine is three units, while a 50ml double shot of spirits is two units, and a pint of lager/cider is two or three, depending on how strong it is).

_____
units a week

Write your weekly figure in here

3
units

2
units

2-3
units

We now know that any amount of alcohol is a health gamble, no matter how small. Given this fact, and the weekly recommended maximum of 14 units a week (at the time of writing this book), how does this figure make you feel?

_____

_____

_____

_____

_____

_____

_____

Now that you know it's actually the norm not to moderate, does that make you feel any better?

_____

_____

_____

_____

_____

_____

the moonshot marketing of alcohol

THE MOST GENIUS MARKETING STRATEGY EVER DEVISED

The marketing machine around alcohol is a dream come true. Imagine you have a new product to roll out to the buying public, and check this out for a moonshot goal of a marketing strategy...

→ People can't have fun without this product.

→ They most certainly can't *dance* without it.

→ This product enables you to get off with people you fancy.

→ This is essential whenever commiserating or celebrating.

→ The product forms the centrepiece of socializing.

→ Despite four-fifths of the population doing it, consuming this product is seen as somehow renegade and rebellious, rather than predictably pedestrian.

→ You use this product both when it's hot and when it's cold.

→ It is an inextricable part of holidays abroad, Christmas, weddings, baby showers, christenings, birthdays, Halloween, bank holidays, Thanksgiving – basically every personal or national celebration.

→ You're only socially approved to stop using this product *if you have to*. Like, if your liver's about to punch itself out of your body and run away to seek sanctuary.

→ If you do manage to stop consuming this, you will be subject to some social scrutiny and suspicion, rather than wide congratulation.

→ People who don't consume this product are thought to be weird, sanctimonious and/or boring.

→ You definitely need to offer visitors this product if they come round to your house.

Now I want to hear from you.

Can you think of any other ways in which the marketing around alcohol is astonishingly successful? What positive attributes are we told sit at the bottom of bottles?

_____

_____

_____

_____

_____

_____

_____

_____

_____

_____

_____

_____

_____

_____

_____

_____

ALCOHOL-GLORIFICATION SCRAPBOOKING

This one will help you stay sane while being assailed by the dozens of pro-drinking messages you will see every dang day.

Here's what I realized, when I was around a year sober. I was giving alcohol-glorification the power to make me feel bad, sad or mad. So, I took that power away from it.

I started approaching the mass glorification of alcohol as if I were an intrepid explorer observing a peculiar tribe's social rituals. I became more objective, more removed, less affected.

I actively looked for pub clapboards, memes, kitsch tin-and-rope signs at vintage fairs; anything with a bizarre pro-boozing message on it. I became like a collector who hunts and rummages for their bounty of choice, except I was collecting booze-a-ganda.

YOUR TASK is to take a picture of every single thing you see, over the next week or so, that is pro-alcohol.

This is a nifty psychological hack. By staying alert, swivelling on your heel, and grabbing these sneaky messages with a 'Gotcha, you little toerag', you will find that these messages can't tiptoe up behind you, knock your feet from under you and put you at risk. You'll disarm and disempower them, rather than finding that they've snuck up, dived into your brain, walked right into your subconscious and have their rude boots up on your table.

Here are just some of the truly wackadoodle things I've seen in shops/advertised recently.

(We can't say who makes these items as our lawyers wouldn't let us.)

Wine glasses that hold an entire bottle of wine

WINE + YOGA

Wine and yoga exercise class

Beer-branded baby bottles

(plus a Champagne-flute baby bottle for the more discerning one-year-old)

Vodka toothpaste

Countless greetings cards, posters, coasters and T-shirts implying that, without alcohol, no-one would ever get laid...

One day, items like these will be in a museum, and future generations will gawp at them and be like, 'No wayyyy. Dude, have you seen this toothpaste?!'
They'll then go home and do essays for homework on how scandalous alcohol glorification was.

YOUR SCRAPBOOK

Full disclosure. I don't *actually* physically 'scrapbook'. I'm a lazy badger, so I tend to just snap pictures of these things on my phone and then send them to my sober mates captioned with searingly insightful commentary such as 'What the actual F, man?!'

Maybe you're less idle than me, and you will scrapbook on these here pages. If so, I salute you.

Or maybe you will just jot down the cuckoo things you see.

Or maybe, if you're arty, you can draw them. Whatever works.

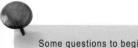

Some questions to begin the dismantling of alcohol-glorification:

1. Are they trying to sell me something (whether it's booze, or something else using the gimmick of booze)?

2. Do I believe marketing messages that imply a car/cleaning product/fitness regime is going to award me a better career, a romantic partner or true happiness?

3. If not, then why would I believe this?

our
mad
world

BIG ALCOHOL IS OMNIPOTENT

Big Alcohol* is incredibly powerful, connected and richer than God.

Just like Big Tobacco was back in the day, when they tried to silence the medical world, when they tried to stifle reports of smoking-related diseases, when they tried to throw money at doctors to bribe them into leading pro-smoking studies.

Every single anti-alcohol headline is an act of valour on the part of the newspaper's/magazine's editor. I know, because I used to work in the press. I have worked on most magazines/newspapers in the UK. And I'm blowing the whistle.

Every publication is influenced by the advertisers that line their salary coffers.

Here's how it goes:

1 Publisher (money person) goes to see editor (words person), having seen today's/this week's/this month's copy. Publisher says we can't say X about alcohol, because Y advertises with us.

2 Editor and publisher have hot words.

3 Editor usually has to tone down the copy, or finish the article on a pro-drinking tilt, so that the alcohol-making advertisers don't pull their big bucks.

4 Editorial does strive to be as independent as possible, but ultimately, until alcohol advertising is banned (please, government, it's about chuffing time), you will never get the full, unbiased, unmuffled story when you pick up a publication that depends on advertising from Big Alcohol.

---

*If I ever die in mysterious circumstances (or *definitely* if I die having been smacked in the head with a vodka bottle) Big Alcohol probably did it. Just saying.

Elsewhere in the world, forward-thinking countries such as Norway, Sweden, Sri Lanka and Malaysia have banned alcohol advertising, either entirely or in huge part.

Over here, our newspapers, magazines and TV stations still depend enormously on alcohol-industry funding.

But, there are clearly some courageous editors out there, because the headlines below are real headlines of the past year, all from highbrow publications. We've come a long way.

Nonetheless, something disturbing is still ever-common. Even if the reportage is unveiling a damning study on alcohol-related deaths or diseases, it will likely still end on a pro-drinking note.

Why?

The omnipotence of Big Alcohol. That's why.

The Daily Telegraph

Drinks industry downplaying cancer risk 'like tobacco giants did'

The New York Times*

Federal agency courted alcohol industry to fund study on benefits of moderate drinking

The Guardian

Even moderate drinking can damage the brain, claim researchers

*If you think I sound like a wild-eyed conspiracy theorist when I tell you that the alcohol industry *pays for doctors to lead studies* that are pro-drinking, take a look at this article, from the *New York Times*, which is freely available online. It's about a $100 million US study that was shut down for this very reason, in 2018.

YOUR PRESS OBSERVATIONS

Over the coming weeks, try keeping an eye out for press about alcohol. Make notes of these articles.

What do they say? What are the facts? (Sort these from the *opinions* expressed, as that's important.)

Observe how the vast majority manage to wrap things up with a pro-drinking message.

ARTICLE/TV SHOW/SIMILAR:

_____

_____

_____

_____

ARTICLE/TV SHOW/SIMILAR:

_____

_____

_____

_____

ARTICLE/TV SHOW/SIMILAR:

_____
_____
_____
_____

ARTICLE/TV SHOW/SIMILAR:

_____
_____
_____
_____

ARTICLE/TV SHOW/SIMILAR:

_____
_____
_____
_____

ARTICLE/TV SHOW/SIMILAR:

_____
_____
_____
_____

HAVE A CONVERSATION WITH AN ALIEN

I often think about how we would explain our mass alcohol use to an alien, given the alien would be a blank slate, with no notion of our societal conditioning, or the normalization of heavy drinking.

My imagined conversation goes like this.

The alien and I are standing watching a strip of bars at kicking-out time.

(Incidentally, my alien looks/sounds a lot like Mike Wazowski from *Monsters Inc.*)

ALIEN: Why are all these people so loud, and falling over?

ME: Because they've drunk something called alcohol. It makes you louder, and encourages stumbling.

ALIEN: Why would people drink such a thing?

ME: Because it soothes social anxiety and can deliver a feel-good buzz.

ALIEN: OK. Why is she crying then?

ME: Oh, it can also make bad things appear bigger than they actually are.

ALIEN: They're not actually considering eating there?!

Gestures to a group of people bee-lining for a ramshackle fast-food joint

ME: Alcohol lowers your culinary standards, dramatically.

ALIEN: Why are those men punching each other?

ME: Ummm, alcohol also dramatically increases physical violence. Out of all evening, night-time and weekend incidents of violence, 70 per cent involve alcohol.

ALIEN: Holy asteroids! Why have humans not outlawed this?!

ME: Because it makes our governments billions of pounds a year, even after they've spent money cleaning up the health problems, crime and so on.

ALIEN: Health problems?

ME: Oh yes, alcohol is a carcinogen, it causes something called cancer, which can often kill you.

ALIEN: This drink can kill you? Do these people not know about the cancer?

ME: Only one in ten of them, says a study.

ALIEN: Why only one in ten? Surely the alcohol comes with health warnings.

ME: Er, no, it doesn't.

ALIEN: What?!

And so on, and so forth. Try it, overleaf, it's a really interesting exercise.

YOUR CONVERSATION
WITH AN ALIEN

WHY 'AM I AN ALCOHOLIC?' IS THE WRONG QUESTION

Back when I was drinking, I spent many late nights, hunched wretchedly over the blue glow of my laptop, typing 'Am I an alcoholic?' into the internet. I did quiz after quiz. Sometimes the internet said I was, sometimes it said I wasn't.

But I was asking the wrong question. I should simply have been asking, 'Would I be happier sober?' And the answer has turned out to be – hell yes!

Our wonky society says that you only quit drinking *if you have to*, rather than *if you want to*. We say things like, 'But I never drink in the morning, so...' (Oh apart from mimosas on holiday, of course) or 'My liver test came back clear, so...'. We're told that you only quit drinking if you're a full-blown alcoholic, who has lost everything and sups meths out of a bottle in a brown paper bag.

That's like saying that you should only consider quitting smoking if you have lung cancer. Or that you only quit your daily gateaux habit if you're clinically obese, or that a nightly cocaine habit is fine as long as you're not snorting it in the loos at work, or that you should only knock your jittery, wired five-a-day coffee habit on the head if you've lost your job due to a coffee-fuelled rant.

Yes, millions of people can drink lashings of alcohol and mostly perform as functioning adults. But being able to function does not mean your alcohol use isn't negatively impacting your life.

I can still walk when I'm carrying a 20kg suitcase, but that doesn't mean I should carry a 20kg suitcase around; that just makes walking harder. And heavy drinking definitely makes life harder.

I do call myself a 'recovering alcoholic', but given I haven't had a drink in five years, I do think it slightly odd. I haven't had a smoke in four years either, but I don't go around saying I'm a 'recovering smokeaholic'. I just no longer smoke.

It's curious that we feel compelled to put ourselves into these boxes. One of the top arguments for the 'alcoholic' label is that it encourages vigilance. But I'm vigilant; I know full well that addictive neural pathways live on in the brain. I know that my 'Let's get so smashed we can't stand!' neural pathway is still there, deep in my head, despite it being disused, dark and choked with weeds. It'll always be there.

I'm here to tell you that there are *no rules*; you don't have to be an 'alcoholic' to quit drinking, any more than you need to be a 'smokeaholic' who smokes 40 a day, to choose to quit smoking.

Nor do you have to call yourself anything, once you've quit. You just don't drink, that's all. Call yourself whatever the heck you like.

I like to say I'm a 'retired hellraiser', as that feels right. (Drinking did indeed feel like a job; now I'm kicking back.)

You choose your own labels, or lack thereof. Nobody else does.

Teetotallers are retired hellraisers. Reformed boozehounds. Mellowed party animals. Not holier-than-thou angels.

@unexpectedjoyof

You can still go to bars.

Only difference is, you'll remember leaving them.

 @unexpectedjoyof

THE SPECTRUM OF DEPENDENT DRINKING

A much more useful way of thinking about dependence on drinking, and one increasingly being used, rather than the traditional black/white, alcoholic/normal drinker dichotomy, is as a spectrum.

The following fun:problems ratio is wildly simplistic, but I heard it in a recovery meeting once, and it helped me enormously. When we start out drinking, normally it's pretty fun, with no visible problems as a result. Over time, as we motor down the scale of dependence, the fun is joined by problems. Then the problems begin to outweigh the fun. Until you're deep into the bottom end of the spectrum, where I got to, where there are – only problems. 'Blast. This is no fun at all, down here.'

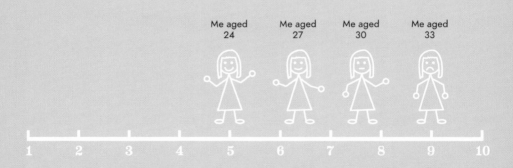

The further down the spectrum you go, the harder it is to quit. There's a recovery saying that if you walk five miles into the woods, remember that you'll have to walk five miles back out. Yup. They nailed it, right there.

Now, I'd like you to position yourself on this blank spectrum, in terms of where you think your most recent drinking would place you.

1   2   3   4   5   6   7   8   9   10

Done that? Cool.

Now, add in a smaller stick-figure you, to denote where you were on this scale three years ago.

Then an even smaller you, for six years ago.

And another, for nine years ago.

Finally, shade the part of the scale that you never, ever want to get to.

What's been happening? What are all the stick-figure yous showing? Have you been sliding further down the scale, as the years roll on by? If so, that's entirely normal.

Sometimes, a life event like pregnancy or a big job promotion, will interrupt the slide, arrest its development, but mostly people slowly, surely, slide further down the spectrum.

Or, there is an alternative: you could just come off the drinking spectrum altogether. If you fancy doing that, draw a picture of the sober stick-figure you below, perhaps with a cup of tea, or surrounded by unicorns, or on a 'Teetotal King' throne, or whatever the blinking hell you like. It's your picture. Go nuts.

@unexpectedjoyof

Alcohol-free
lagoon.
Jump in.

FEEL FREE TO SNAP AND SHARE ON INSTAGRAM/TWITTER/FACEBOOK.
IF YOU'RE NOT ON THE SOCIALS (RESPECT!), CUT IT OUT, PUT IT IN YOUR WALLET, WHATEVER WORKS.

Your weekends get so much bigger
when you ditch booze.

 @unexpectedjoyof

sober/
drinking
splitscreening

WEEKEND SPLITSCREENS

Sober weekends *are* big and they *are* clever.

You don't lose mornings to sleeping off hangovers, you have the energy to do productive, mind-enriching adult things like going to exhibitions, reading books, re-decorating, doing the things you said you were going to do.

You'll roll into Monday feeling rested and recharged. I used to limp into Mondays feeling like I should be going to hospital, rather than to my workplace.

The best way to see the many blindingly obvious, or subtle (yet powerful) differences, is to sit your sober/drinking weekends side by side.

DRINKING WEEKEND   SOBER WEEKEND

_____   _____

_____   _____

_____   _____

_____   _____

_____   _____

_____   _____

_____   _____

_____   _____

DRINKING WEEKEND

SOBER WEEKEND

_____

_____

_____

_____

_____

_____

_____

_____

_____

_____

_____

_____

_____

_____

_____

_____

_____

_____

_____

DRINKING WEEKEND

_____
_____
_____
_____
_____
_____
_____
_____
_____
_____
_____
_____
_____
_____
_____
_____
_____
_____
_____

SOBER WEEKEND

_____
_____
_____
_____
_____
_____
_____
_____
_____
_____
_____
_____
_____
_____
_____
_____
_____
_____
_____

DRINKING WEEKEND

_____

_____

_____

_____

_____

_____

_____

_____

_____

_____

_____

_____

_____

_____

_____

_____

_____

SOBER WEEKEND

_____

_____

_____

_____

_____

_____

_____

_____

_____

_____

_____

_____

_____

_____

_____

_____

_____

Teetotal holidays.
You won't need a
holiday to recover
from your holiday.

@unexpectedjoyof

FEEL FREE TO SNAP AND SHARE ON INSTAGRAM/TWITTER/FACEBOOK.
IF YOU'RE NOT ON THE SOCIALS (RESPECT!), CUT IT OUT, PUT IT IN YOUR WALLET, WHATEVER WORKS.

WHY SOBRIETY IS LIKE THE MARSHMALLOW EXPERIMENT

Have you heard of the Stanford Marshmallow Experiment? Back in the 1960s a bunch of scientists took 600 kids and used thousands of marshmallows to explore delayed gratification.

They sat the kids in a room, in front of one marshmallow on a plate, and offered them a choice. Either they could eat one marshmallow right now, or they could wait 15 minutes to get two.

Cue the kids doing hilarious things like sitting with their back to the marshmallow, stroking it as if it were a hamster or scrutinizing it from every possible angle.

Around one-third of the 600 kids waited for the helping of double marshmallows.

They tracked the 600 throughout their lives and found that the ones who opted for delayed, double gratification, tended to have better SAT scores, a healthier BMI and similar life wins.

When I first read about this experiment, in my twenties, delayed gratification was such an alien, Spock-like concept to me, that I was dumbfounded that anyone waited. 'What's wrong with you, kid?! Take that marshmallow and stuff it in your mouth, pronto! What are you, a psychopath?'

But now, I've finally learned that reaching for instant, smaller gratification is foolish.

Sobriety is exactly the same as the marshmallow experiment, since it's about training yourself to be the kid who's wise enough to deny instant gratification and waits for the double rewards.

Drinking is one marshmallow. It's answering the call of want-it-now. It's giving into 'Gimme' discomfort and desire. Whereas teetotalling is double marshmallows; sitting on your hands, doing the harder, but smarter thing. Knowing that long-term bigger picture trumps short-term smaller picture.

Write here about the short-term sacrifices, and long-term rewards, of what you're doing.

SHORT-TERM SACRIFICE

LONG-TERM REWARDS

_____

_____

_____

_____

_____

_____

_____

_____

_____

_____

_____

_____

SHORT-TERM SACRIFICE

_____

_____

_____

_____

_____

_____

_____

_____

_____

_____

_____

_____

_____

_____

LONG-TERM REWARDS

_____

_____

_____

_____

_____

_____

_____

_____

_____

_____

_____

_____

_____

_____

Serene, lovely and smooth.
That's how long-term sober feels.

@unexpectedjoyof

We're meant to drink things that rehydrate us.

Not things that dehydrate us.

This guy knows.

 @unexpectedjoyof

the
physical
wins

Once you're a couple of weeks into teetotalling and your body has started to mend deep down, you should start to experience the exquisite deliciousness of sober sleep.

Pre-quitting, this is what my sleep looked like. I could sleep (read: pass out) when batfaced, obviously, but I would conk out, clothes half-on, smeared clown make-up staining my pillow, for ten to eleven hours. And *still* wake up at midday on a Sunday knackered, feeling like a zombie, hangdog guilty about squandering hours and hours of the morning.

Then, the next night, when I was hungover and not drinking (and thus going through low-level withdrawal) it would get even worse.

I would stare at the ceiling, doomscaping, tossing and turning until 3/4am, freaking out about not being rested for work. When I finally slumbered, I would have regular nightmares about being chased, wake up five or six times, drink water beside bed due to chronic dehydration, knock over water beside bed, have to clean up water beside bed.

And the finale: hit snooze on my 7:45am alarm four times and finally haul myself out of bed feeling like a seventy-year-old, despite being a twentysomething. Monday night's sleep would be much better, but on Tuesday I would generally hit the pub and the whole cycle of horribly unsatisfying smashed/hungover sleep would start again.

It's deeply ironic that millions of people use booze as a sleeping aid, since it actually screws with our natural ability to sleep. Alcohol prevents us from going into restorative REM sleep, which is when our brain learns and beds in memories. The National Sleep Foundation says that REM sleep is 'thought to be involved in the process of storing memories, learning and balancing our mood'.

What's more, there's ample scientific evidence that REM sleep is when your brain takes the bins out, disposing of unnecessary clutter, thus making room for new and important information. A 2017 paper entitled 'Sleep is for forgetting' concluded that 'sleep is essential for the targeted, careful forgetting necessary for experience-dependent synaptic circuit reshaping during development and throughout the lifespan'. In layman's terms, REM sleep is a marvellous, necessary waste-disposal system, and without it, our brains grow clogged and confused.

Basically, REM sleep is when your brain gets its shit together, so that it's ready to roll the next day. And the best way you can help it get there is by going to sleep non-hungover and sober.

On top of all of that, when you're drinking, your body/brain will prioritize more addictive booze over getting to bed at a sensible time. I used to think that I was staying up/out until 2am because I simply had to continue this life-changing conversation, or I wanted to go dancing!, or that I was gripped by the twisty-turny TV crime drama I was bingeing on.

Actually, if there'd been no more alcohol to be had, I would have gone home/turned in, so the thing keeping me up was the alcohol, not the conversation/nightclub/TV show. *I stayed up late to drink more.* This became abundantly clear after just a few weeks of sobriety, given I pretty much always wanted to head to bed by midnight.

I remain utterly gobsmacked by sober sleep. That I can put my head on the pillow, sail off into inky seas within twenty minutes, and usually don't stir until eight hours later, when I wake up with a mind that's as clear and tranquil as a still pool.

It's sensational. You'll soon see.

YOUR SOBER SLEEP
EXPERIENCE DIARY

What was your drunk sleep like?

_____
_____
_____
_____
_____
_____
_____

What was your hungover, non-drinking-night sleep like?

_____
_____
_____
_____
_____
_____
_____

DESCRIBE FOUR NIGHTS OF SOBER SLEEP:

(after at least a fortnight of sobriety, since the first couple of weeks of sober sleep can be restless, while your body adjusts. My blissed-out sober sleep kicked in after three weeks, but I drank a lot before my quit date, so your slumber might start to settle earlier.)

NIGHT ONE:

_____

_____

_____

_____

_____

_____

NIGHT TWO:

_____

_____

_____

_____

_____

_____

NIGHT THREE:

_____

_____

_____

_____

_____

NIGHT FOUR:

_____

_____

_____

_____

_____

What conclusions do you draw, now that you've compared drinking and hungover vs. sober sleep?

_____

_____

_____

_____

_____

FOOD DIARIES

Another unexpected side effect of sobriety was what I ate.

 You'll naturally crave more nutritious food. No effort required.

 You'll crave fewer salty snacks, now that you're no longer viciously dehydrated (chronic dehydration triggers a craving for salt, oddly enough).

 On the flipside, you'll notice an enhanced sweet tooth, given you're no longer consuming the many spoonfuls of sugar hidden in most types of booze (even beer).

 You never experience that ferocious 'I could eat a rhino' hangover hunger.

HUNGOVER ME

BREAKFAST: Three coffees to make up for chronic lack of sleep, plus either a ham and cheese croissant, or if I felt extra rancid, a coke and a sausage roll.

LUNCH: The biggest baguette I could find, a behemoth I could barely carry out of the shop.

SNACK: Crisps. Monster Munch, if possible.

DINNER: If I was in, it would be a ready-made cottage pie or lasagne that you whack in the oven, as I would be bone-tired from my hangover and too knackered to cook. If I was out again, it would normally be greasy pizza or questionable chicken and chips on the way home.

SOBER ME

BREAKFAST: Porridge with hazelnut milk, cinnamon, coconut and blueberries.

LUNCH: Salmon, avocado and eggs, or tuna fishcake and greens.

SNACK: Chocolate biscuits dunked in tea, almonds, or a homemade mango and banana smoothie.

DINNER: Prawns, feta, couscous and salad. Or veggie fajitas. Followed by vanilla ice cream, toasted coconut and strawberries.

TYPICAL HUNGOVER DAY

_____

_____

_____

_____

_____

_____

_____

_____

TYPICAL SOBER DAY

_____

_____

_____

_____

_____

_____

_____

_____

TYPICAL HUNGOVER DAY

_____

_____

_____

_____

_____

_____

_____

TYPICAL SOBER DAY

_____

_____

_____

_____

_____

_____

_____

TYPICAL HUNGOVER DAY

_____

_____

_____

_____

_____

_____

_____

TYPICAL SOBER DAY

_____

_____

_____

_____

_____

_____

_____

TYPICAL HUNGOVER DAY

_____

_____

_____

_____

_____

_____

_____

_____

TYPICAL SOBER DAY

_____

_____

_____

_____

_____

_____

_____

_____

YOUR PHYSICAL TRANSFORMATION

Before and after pictures are powerful. Not just because they allow you to see how much better you look sober, but also because you'll see how much happier you are.

We're going to do something radical. Something rarely done in today's society. Bear with me. (Millennials, fair warning: your heads might explode.)

We are going to *print out some photos*. Rather than leave them trapped in our computers/phones. And then we're going to cut them out, and stick them to this page, like actual art-and-crafters.

It's totally up to you whether you actually go to the faff of having these printed onto photo paper by professionals, or whether you go down my preferred idle route of copying and pasting pics onto a word document and then using a colour printer.

DINNERS

Before

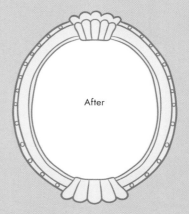

After

Here I felt:
_____
_____
_____

Here I felt:
_____
_____
_____

NIGHTS OUT

Before

After

Here I felt:
_____
_____
_____

Here I felt:
_____
_____
_____

MORNINGS

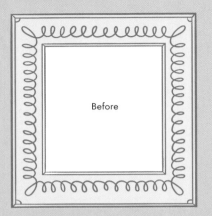

Before

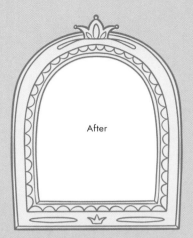

After

Here I felt:

_____

_____

_____

Here I felt:

_____

_____

_____

DAYS OUT

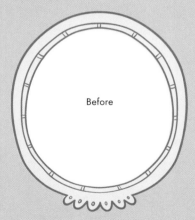

Before

After

Here I felt:

_____

_____

_____

Here I felt:

_____

_____

_____

LUST-O-METER

There's nothing sexy about sex you can't remember.

@unexpectedjoyof

Drama.
Life inevitably has less of it when you don't drink.

@unexpectedjoyof

PHYSICAL CHANGES DIARY

Here, we're going to write down all of the little ways you start to feel, smell and look different. It's not just about looks; it's about how you feel too.

So your skin may look better, for sure – mine most certainly did – but it was just as satisfying that it felt less parched, too, and more silky.

Or, your dandruff/itchy scalp might go away, but you may also find it incredibly satisfying that your hair no longer smells like *Tiger Tiger*.

Meanwhile, underneath your hair, you may stop getting migraines, since alcohol is a chronic cause of them, given it increases blood flow to the brain, and not in a good way.

Your back may well be less dotted with blemishes, but it also may feel more fluid and less crunchy, given drinking can cause a lactic acid build-up, which leads to muscular knots and cramps.

Your chest may stop flushing now that you don't drink, while your heartrate may lower to a healthier pace.

Your waist may well lose inches now that you're not quaffing empty calories, but you may also notice that your stomach is less gassy and more settled.

Meanwhile, the lower half of your body may experience changes such as better digestive movements or even sweeter-smelling feet (it's a thing).

Start keeping this diary once you're at least a month in, since it takes a good few weeks for these changes to start to kick in. This is why I always recommend at least three months off booze to really start to reap the physical wins.

HAIR/HEAD:

FACE:

_____

_____

_____

_____

_____

_____

_____

_____

BACK/CHEST:

_____

_____

_____

_____

_____

_____

_____

_____

WAIST/STOMACH:

_____

_____

_____

_____

_____

_____

_____

_____

LOWER HALF OF BODY:

_____

_____

_____

_____

_____

_____

_____

_____

Bad day?

It won't turn into a bad month if you *just stay dry.*

 @unexpectedjoyof

when life gives you lemons

TEETOTAL ANGER MANAGEMENT

Once I quit drinking, I experienced a lightbulb moment; a realization very common among the newly sober. Much of my drinking was powered by anger. I drank *at* people.

If somebody peed me off, I would deal with it by going to the pub with my mates and ranting (sorry mates), while they fired up my ire further by siding with me, or tried to calm me down by tentatively suggesting I be more magnanimous/look on the bright side (which only served to make me even more mad).

Or, if I had no mates/no family member to bore, I would down wine at home, muttering like the Tasmanian devil about what a dipshit [insert person] is, and scripting imaginary arguments in my head, which I always won, obviously.

When I sobered up, I needed a new way to deal with anger, other than deep-diving into wine. Because, guess what? Like the Buddhists say, holding onto anger is like clutching a red-hot coal, a coal intended for the other person. You're only burning yourself. Or, as the recovery saying goes, it's like 'drinking poison and expecting the other person to die'. (Given alcohol is a neurotoxin, this is actually pretty bang-on.) You're trying to exact revenge on *them*, but the only person you're hurting is *yourself*.

But you're allowed to be angry. You're a human being, not an error-free android, and anger is an inextricable part of the human experience. Trying *never to be angry* is an impossible mission. So, let's lean into this entirely human anger, rather than shove it away, and sort through it, shall we?

We'll start with a wholesome colouring exercise.

PENNING A 'FUCK YOU!' LETTER

Can't be arsed to colour stuff in? I hear you, I'm a writer rather than a colour-inner. So, when I am furious with someone, I tend to write a 'Fuck You!' letter. A letter that I will never send, of course.

It's purely for cathartic purposes, to stop me snapping randomly at the person in question, and to release the repetitive script that is looping around in my head.

Try it, here!

(Go to town. Don't hold back. Really tear strips off them. Do your worst. Say the darkest things that you're thinking.)

I bet you a hundred golden coins that if you hang onto the 'Fuck You!' letter and read it again in a fortnight, you'll be somewhat perplexed as to why you felt such white-hot rage. Because of this, a 'Fuck You!' letter revisit always reassures me that I move through feelings like weather; they're not permanent.

Dear [insert person] _____,

I love you /usually like you/always mildly dislike you
[delete as appropriate]

But today, I am really fucking mad at you, and I need to let that out, so that I don't try to anaesthetize it with a bottle of alcohol. Here's what is swirling around inside my angry head:

_____

_____

_____

_____

_____

_____

_____

_____

_____

_____

_____

_____

_____

_____

_____

_____

WRITING A
'THANK YOU' LETTER

Here's the thing with 'Fuck You!' letters. Once you see all of that venom, all of that anger down in black and white, you also get some perspective, some distance, some calm. You can start to see that this mean-spirited (but entirely human and permitted) missive does not reflect the whole truth.

You may generally dislike your boss, OK, but there was *that time when*, or *that other time when* [insert positive thing]. Also, they gave you a job, yes? Which enables you to buy food, no?

You may not be cut from the same kinda cloth as your best mate's mum/your mother-in-law, and may actively disagree with most of the things she says, but she made your best mate/partner, right? So, that was good of her.

That family member who's doing your nut in? Don't you also love things about them?

So, after I write a 'Fuck You!' letter to someone, I close up the anger circle neatly by writing a 'Thank You' letter to the same person, in which I acknowledge all the things that are good about them. All the things I'm grateful for. You will be able to find those things, if you hunt high and low.

This leaves me in a lovely, peaceful state of mind. I've stopped drinking the poison. I've let go of the scorching coal. And most of all, I've done myself a colossal favour.

Give it a whirl...

Dear [insert person] _____,

I'm still fucked off with you, for sure, but I acknowledge that there is no such thing as a perfect person, nor a person who behaves exactly as I want them to (until I can purchase and pre-programme convincing robots. And even then, they always, always rebel in films, so...).

I realize I can't control you; I can only control how I react to you.

Here are the things I like about you, plus the things you have previously done that I am thankful for.

_____

_____

_____

_____

_____

_____

_____

_____

_____

_____

_____

_____

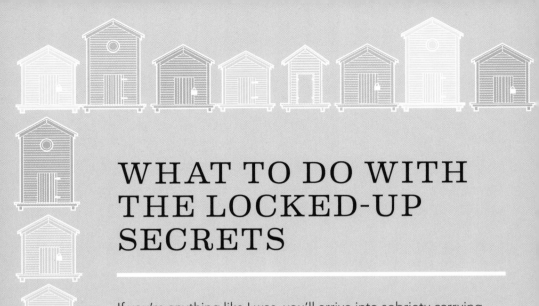

WHAT TO DO WITH THE LOCKED-UP SECRETS

If you're anything like I was, you'll arrive into sobriety carrying a huge backpack of secrets and shame; baggage from your drinking days.

Here's the thing about being drunk. That's not who you are. The reason drunk people often do things they would never dream of doing sober, is because they are under the influence of a mind-altering drug. It's like a capricious, reckless, lustful, food-obsessed brat has bodysnatched you for the night. A friend used to call my drunken alter ego 'snog demon', which neatly summed it up.

And when you're blackout drunk? Man oh man. The lights may appear to be on, given you can walk (stagger), talk (slur repetitively) and make decisions (terrible ones), but the wise parts of your brain have gone home, and the show is being directed by the most primitive part of your brain. The hippocampus can no longer store memories for more than half an hour, which is why you remember *nothing of this horrifying performance* come the morning.

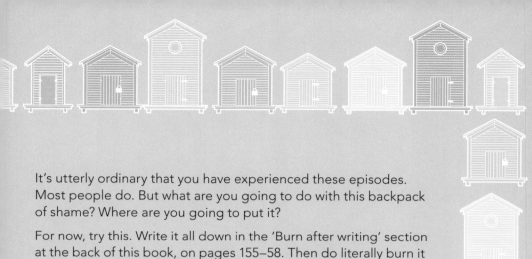

It's utterly ordinary that you have experienced these episodes. Most people do. But what are you going to do with this backpack of shame? Where are you going to put it?

For now, try this. Write it all down in the 'Burn after writing' section at the back of this book, on pages 155–58. Then do literally burn it (disclaimer: in a safe way, don't torch your town down).

Try to forgive yourself. That wasn't the real you. This is. Your sober actions reflect your actual values. Your true character is uncovered when you're drug-free, not when you're wankered on a drink that makes half your brain shut down.

Long-term, you might eventually want to share the backpack with a (very) trusted friend or a therapist. I have. But I did that when I was well over three years sober, when I felt entirely ready to do so, and when I knew for a fact that my secrets would remain safe with her.

People can change. They do, all the blooming time. Into entirely different people. Especially once they've stopped taking a drug that perverts their values and personality.

One of the best things about sobering up was finding out who I actually was. Finding out that I wasn't a terrible friend, or a natural-born liar, or a work-dodger who called in sick constantly, or incapable of being faithful in a romantic relationship. I became who I was always destined to be before drinking threw me off course. You will too.

Your real self is your sober self.

Alcohol plunders
you of health, money
and self-esteem.
Chuck it overboard.

@unexpectedjoyof

SLIP
PREVENTION

It's incredibly normal to have a slip-slidey time when you first attempt to quit drinking.

Personally, I experienced five months of stop – start – stop – start. 99.9 per cent of people do not hit a home run the moment they pick up the bat.

I would manage to string seven days together, like delicate daisies on a chain, and whoosh! they'd be whipped away. And I'd sit there, looking at my empty chain, crying.

The secret is, shake it off and try again. And again. And again. Until it sticks. As Einstein said, 'You never fail until you stop trying'. F. Scott Fitzgerald got 122 rejection slips before selling his first story.

It's like conquering a computer game. Each attempt, you learn more, get further, finesse your skills, until: Eureka! She/he's got it.

In the picture above, I'm paddle-boarding in the Philippines. You may notice I'm sitting down, rather than standing up. That's because every time I stood up, I slipped and fell in. So I just stopped standing up. If a certain thing keeps making you slip and fall into the water, or wobble significantly, simply stop doing it for now. Learn the feel of being on the board, the paddle, get your balance, before trying to stand again.

Each boozy slip contains a valuable lesson. Did you meet up with someone who didn't know you're not drinking, thus greeted you with a glass of fizz? Did you go on a pre-booked stag do in your first month sober? Did you swerve your HIIT class after a dreadful day when you could have really used that punchbag station, and instead made a bee-line for the wine aisle?

Take that lesson and learn from it. Change up how you approach this situation next time. The best advice I've ever had about slipping is 'Don't try harder. Try different.'

So, you had a drink. I know you're disappointed and I'm sorry.
Was it worth it? Did it give you what you felt you needed?

_____

_____

What happened to lead you to that drink?

_____

_____

What will you do differently next time?

_____

_____

_____

Whatever sensation you were looking for in that bottle
(relaxation, relief, whatever it was), how could you achieve
that via an alcohol-free activity?

_____

_____

_____

You are not a failure. You are trying to do an exceptionally difficult thing, that most people don't even attempt. Your slip does not undo the days you had before it. Now hop back on, giddy up and let's ride on.

The best things
in life take time.

Effort.

Big-picture thinking.

@unexpectedjoyof

Sobriety.

Fewer cheap thrills. But more dignity.

@unexpectedjoyof

I don't
get smashed
anymore

your newfound wealth

GET-SOLVENT-QUICK

You'll be astonished at how much money a drinking habit snaffles, and therefore how much more you have now. In my five years of sobriety, my money-saved counting app (*I'm done drinking*) tells me that I have saved over £35K.

This is because I was spending around £135 a week on alcohol, and the subsequent trappings of alcohol. (No wonder I was always bloody skint.)

I know that sounds like *a lot*, but here's how it ticks up. Two nights out at the pub per week? £25 each if you include the homeward-bound fast food. Lob in one 3am taxi. Chuck in three more nights of drinking at home: £14 per night on Sauvignon Blanc 'n' ten Vogue menthols. Then throw in two nights off boozing, but with expenses due to hangover spends (the film bought on Amazon + the takeaway), and you've easily reached £135.

Thanks to that ginormous saving, I've managed to pay off over £10K of debt; I never ever get charged now for tipping over the precipice of my overdraft (I don't even have an overdraft, nor do I live on the cliff-edge of it); I am now a total files-tax-return-five-months-early swot. I even have an accountant forgodsake. As a result, my credit rating has tipped over from a scorchy red (do not touch this person!) to a satisfying, leafy green (have a picnic with this person!).

I've done my PADI open-water diving qualification in the Philippines, I've enjoyed a road trip from New Orleans to San Francisco, and many more trips besides to Antigua, Prague, Paris, and so on. I've spent seven months living in Bruges and three months living in Barcelona while in between rental leases. I have sold two iPhones on eBay because they have been in such good nick that I could (pre-sober I always dropped them down pub toilets/smashed my phones on the Soho floor and constantly had to replace them).

I've finally done driving lessons aged 38 and have officially failed my first driving test (whoop!), I've bought my first-ever actual furniture from eBay, Ikea and vintage fairs. I've moved from house-sharing with three others in London to having my own fourth-floor Brighton bolthole; the sunset paints itself across the window like an invisible artist working on an easel. My little flat can just about see the sea if it stands on its tiptoes.

I mean, I haven't actually saved anything or got a pension yet, and the closest I am to owning property is the dusty Smurf Castle in my parents' attic, but… details. Let's move swiftly on, shall we? Full financial recovery + learning how to save: pending ;-) I'm still colossally better off than I was five years ago.

Before you go thinking I'm a trust-fund baby, I did all of the above when I was earning closer to £20K than £30K a year. On top of which, I'm a financial nitwit. Truly. I have the financial mental age of a fourteen-year-old. People openly laugh at me when I unveil my woeful knowledge about ISAs and pensions and APR.

So if I can clear my debt, indulge my wanderlust, buy furniture, sell my used iPhones and change my credit rating thanks to teetotalling, *you most definitely can.*

What are you gonna spend all your spare money on?

First things first, let's work out how much you spend/spent on booze per week. I'm not just talking about the physical bottles or the actual bar tabs, I'm also talking about all of the inevitable offshoot expenses. These include:

THE NIGHT OF

- [ ] Tipsy online shopping sprees
- [ ] Whisky-sour-fuelled gambling flutters
- [ ] Nightclub entry
- [ ] Naughty fags bought after a few
- [ ] 1am trips to the golden arches/ your local curry house
- [ ] Any items lost/broken during nightcrawls (including phone, umbrella, jacket, wallet, bag, laptop)
- [ ] Taxis when you miss the last bus/train

THE DAY AFTER

- [ ] Missed gym session/exercise class (especially if it incurs a Classpass style fine for non-attendance)
- [ ] Deliveroo/takeaways because you're too hungover to cook
- [ ] Spontaneous boxset/film buy so that you can legitimately lie on sofa for hours
- [ ] If you're freelance, add in a lost day of work

_____ per week

OK, have you got your week's figure? Good. I know, it's depressing. I'm sorry. But now multiply it by four. Eep. Even more startling.

But here's some good news. You are now NOT SPENDING that money, therefore you can spend it on bodacious stuff instead. Ker-ching.

Insert that monthly saving amount into the treasure chest below.

per
month

I have a very important task for you. This is compulsory, OK?

One of the classic mistakes most people make when they quit drinking is that they don't replace the 'treat' of drinking with other life-sweetening treats. Thus, their teetotalling starts to feel fricking boring and a lot like deprivation.

They swerve the night at the pub, or picking up a bottle on the way home, and don't insert something lovely in its place, thus life does indeed start to feel grey. Course it does.

YOUR TASK is to spend at least half of what you are saving on little sober treats, all the while mindfully noticing that this treat is a reward for not pouring alcohol into yourself. Also, this treat is something your drinking perhaps stopped you from being able to afford.

Now, have a think about what you want. A book, a gadget, a posh candle, entry to a photography exhibition, a £25 hack through leafy woods on a horse, a life-drawing class, a day trip to a new place; think of all those things you want to have/do, but never get/do.

Insert your figures for different boozy scenarios opposite, and then think of lots of specific ways in which that money could be better spent.

SWITCH UP:

One night's drinking-at-home

🐷 _____

FOR: _____

_____

_____

_____

_____

_____

SWITCH UP:

An out-out bender of a night

🐷 _____

FOR: _____

_____

_____

_____

_____

_____

SWITCH UP:

A month of hangovers

🐷 _____

FOR: _____

_____

_____

_____

_____

_____

SWITCH UP:

A year of drinking

🐷 _____

FOR: _____

_____

_____

_____

_____

_____

Excited yet, about how much further your money will go? You should be!

A book costs the same as a bottle of wine.

One shrinks the brain (literally).

The other expands it.

@unexpectedjoyof

FEEL FREE TO SNAP AND SHARE ON INSTAGRAM/TWITTER/FACEBOOK.
IF YOU'RE NOT ON THE SOCIALS (RESPECT!), CUT IT OUT, PUT IT IN YOUR WALLET, WHATEVER WORKS.

Quitting
drinking is
like quitting
smoking.

Long-term,
you feel free.
Uncaged.

O @unexpectedjoyof

the
future is
teetotal

NON-DRINKERS
ARE THE NEW
NON-SMOKERS

I know, right?! Those are *real*.
It's hard to believe, but it happened.

The way non-drinkers are treated socially is nothing new. It's an exact echo of how non-smokers were treated a couple of decades ago.

In the nineties and noughties, people started quitting smoking in their droves. My first friends who quit smoking (having seen the light long before the rest of us) were denounced as smug and sanctimonious, 'killjoys' and 'health bores', by the rest of us. We tried to topple their attempts by offering them fags, like the crabs who pull escaping crabs back into the bucket. 'No! If I'm staying here, you are too!'

Why did we behave this way? Purely because their non-smoking held up an uncomfortable mirror to our smoking. It was about us, not them.

DRINKING WILL BECOME OPT-IN, RATHER THAN OPT-OUT

The latest figures show that those aged 16–24 (or 'Generation Sensible' as the press has nicknamed them) are the least likely to drink, of any age group. A colossal 29 per cent of them now don't drink, ever. Traditionally, this age group was normally the one that drank the most, lashing it up in nightclubs, keeping the lights on in student dive bars across the nation.

Back in 2005, only 18 per cent of 16–24-year-olds were teetotal. Something big has shifted. Drinking clearly isn't appealing to them – which is a very interesting indicator of what the future might look like.

Within the next couple of decades, I reckon the majority of Brits will switch to being alcohol-free. Drinking will no longer be the default, therefore it'll be more of an 'opt-in' rather than an 'opt-out' affair.

Remember when you ticked 'non-smoker' on the first dating apps, way back in the noughties? Now we don't even specify, because non-smoking is the norm, by far. Being a 'non-drinker' will become similarly redundant as a descriptor, as society evolves. Defining yourself by the absence of something, by the non-participation in something, is a bit odd anyway. I wouldn't call myself a 'non-gymnast' or a 'non-vaper'.

Non-drinkers are simply the new non-smokers. Those who are not drinking right now, whether for six nights a week, for three months, or for life, are the trailblazers, the torchbearers running ahead of the pack.

Just like those who quit fags when it was still socially acceptable to blow smoke in each other's faces in the pub. When it was still OK to chain smoke while somebody tried to enjoy a meal a few feet away (which was only outlawed in 2007 in Britain, believe it or not).

VEGANS ARE WEIRD

Another parallel is veganism. I remember when veganism was seen as the exclusive choice of a fervent few. They were regarded as nutcases; everyone wisecracked about them only eating apples that lobbed themselves from the tree, or 'But what if this carrot has feelings, though?'

Now, veganism is utterly mainstream, and the biggest-booming section of the food industry. The vegans that we derided back in the nineties were simply ahead of their time, lighthouses that we would soon look to, frontrunners of a social revolution.

If Western countries do become mostly teetotal, I think it will do the opposite to what is expected for our nightlife. Yes, many dismal little pubs will close, I'm sure. But given I now spend a damn-sight more on gigs, theatre, gorgeous food and going to exhibitions, simply because I have the money to do so, I believe a less-boozy world could see a huge wealth injection into the arts.

Our nightlife could become more vibrant, more exciting and more imaginative. Because being sober sure as hell does not mean staying in for the rest of your life. I go out *more* now than I did in the last years of my drinking.

ALAS, I NEED TO BID YOU FAREWELL

Now it's entirely up to you what you choose, where you go and how you proceed. If you're game for an entirely alcohol-free future, then I'm delighted for you. Whereas, if you want to shoot for 80 per cent sober, then by all means give it a bash, and I genuinely hope it works out.

Because that's the point, isn't it. Your non-drinking, or drinking, is entirely your choice. You get to choose what you put/don't put into your body. Now that you've learnt how to be 100 per cent sober, that's always a viable option, should moderation not work out. It's always here for you. But whatever you do, if you do drink, make sure it's your decision, rather than one you're press-ganged into.

It doesn't matter one little tiny whit what anyone else thinks about your decision to not imbibe a depressant. It doesn't matter if your mother wants you to have wine with dinner again, or if your mates think you 'need to let your hair down' with after-work cocktails, or if your partner misses 7pm G&Ts with you. That's about them. This is about you.

What matters is how *you* feel. If you feel better sober, then you deserve to be sober. I used to think I deserved to drink, but now I see I'd merely been programmed to think that. I was just a brainwashed product of millions of pro-drinking and anti-sobriety messages. Given how much better my life is alcohol-free, I know now that I actually deserve *not* to drink.

Maybe you feel the same. Maybe you don't. We're not the same person, so you make up your own mind. Either way, you should be proud of yourself, given you've done some thinking about your drinking, rather than staying swaddled in the denial duvet.

Whatever you choose, whatever your quest, whatever your next step is, know this; I'm rooting for you.

If you're happier
SOBER,
you don't 'deserve'
A DRINK.
YOU DESERVE
NOT TO
have a drink.

@unexpectedjoyof

TE
A MO
MAMA
♡

Don't forget to thank
those who have helped.

The helpers are golden.

 @unexpectedjoyof

SNAP & SHARE

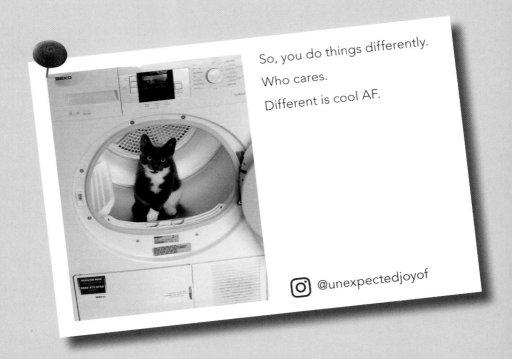

So, you do things differently.

Who cares.

Different is cool AF.

@unexpectedjoyof

BURN AFTER WRITING

Read pages 128–29 and then spill all of your drinking/hungover secrets and shame onto these pages. Then tear/cut them out and burn them.

BURN AFTER WRITING

BURN AFTER WRITING

BURN AFTER WRITING